Fields with God

Wirtten and Illustrated by Lorraine Curry
—with Jean Hall—

Fields with God

Book design, layout and illustration—Lorraine Curry

Editing—Jean Hall

Field Guide—Jon Farrar, *Field Guide to Wildflowers of Nebraska and the Great Plains* (Lincoln: Nebraska Library Commission, *NEBRASKAland Magazine,* Game and Parks Commission; 1990).
    Field Guide
    NEBRASKAland Magazine
    PO Box 30370
    Lincoln NE 68503

"SpillMilk" — Ethan/www.fonthead.com

Fields with God

Easter 2010

To Gail –
who loves God's
handwork as much
as I do –
love
Sheila

God's Gardener
Boelus NE 68820 USA

The little cares which fretted me,
I lost them yesterday
Among the fields, above the sea,
Among the winds at play,
Among the lowing of the herds,
The rustling of the trees,
Among the singing of the birds,
The humming of the bees.

The foolish fears of what may come,
I cast them all away,
Among the clover-scented grass,
Among the new-mown hay;
Among the hushing of the corn,
Where drowsing poppies nod,
Ill thoughts can die and good are born—
Out in the fields of God.

—Anonymous

Stevenson, Burton, Egbert, *The Home Book of Verse*. This poem has also been said to have been written by Elizabeth Barrett Browning or Louise Imogen Guiney.

Thank You

Jean Hall

I greatly appreciate your help with all of our books!

Fields with God
Easy Homeschooling Techniques Christian Edition
Easy Homeschooling Companion
Easy Homeschooling Techniques General Edition

Dedicated, with love, to my children:

Jessica Curry Jobes
Zephi Curry
Ezra Curry
Eli Curry

Arise, go forth into the plain, and I will
there talk with thee. —Ezekiel 3:22

Contents

Preface . . . 9

Summer . . . 11

• The Oak Trees • A Different World • Eastern Kingbird • God Plants My Garden • The Petal Heart • The Hollyhock • The Daylily • His Gifts • Letting God Do It • Cut The Dead Trees Down • He Loves Me! • Peter Rabbit • Our Shepherd • It's Okay • Draw Near to God • The Black Bird • Change • Wild Turkeys Teach • Morning Guilds the Skies • Decide to Be Happy • Birds, Sun, Quiet and Money

Fall and Winter . . . 51

• Sometimes, It's Fall • Be Still • A Day Off • Weekend! • The Squirrel • Seasons • The Wilderness • Snowy Day, Late Winter • Blessed • Purpose • Mother's Heart • Daughter of God! • Strength Attracts • The End • Blowing in from the Sea

Spring . . . 79

• The Porch Swing • Prayer • Dream Dreams • A Personal God • Green Pastures • Priorities • Deep Roots • Free! • Peace • Still Waters • The Baby Cardinal • Use Your Senses • Rushing Grasses • Come Away • Thankfulness from Murmuring

The Mother Tree . . . 107

• The Mother Tree • Bone of my Bones • Our Thoughts • Immovable
• Older Children • Different but Similar • Think Green • Dried and
Dead? • Be Thankful • New Growth! • Regrets • Call Unto Me • Thy
Maker is Thy Husband

Preface

As a homeschooling parent, my children were my life. It was extremely difficult when each left the nest, especially when the youngest—two sons— seemed to leave at the same time. Fortunately, before these things happened, God had taken us out of town and moved us to the country, setting us down on forty gorgeous acres. It is here, *in the fields*, that God meets me and heals me, giving me power to overcome and bright hope for the future.

I've arranged this book by the seasons and summer is undoubtedly my favorite season. How could one not love the warmth, the sun, the growth, the flowers, the fireflies, the green, the nights of summer?!

God also wants our lives to also have mostly "summer" chapters.

These pages are God's gift to me, and I pass them on to you. May you find encouragement for the "down" days we all seem to have, even hope in the blackest night. May you know the perfect unconditional love of God for you, and may you know, really know, one more very powerful thing—

God is everywhere.

He is in you, in your relationships, in your children, in your DNA, in your bones, in your eyes, in your heart, in your home, outside your home, surrounding your body, in the city, in airplanes, in vehicles, on the interstate, in stores, around the people you love, in the trees, in the soft breeze that whispers your name, in animals and . . . *in the fields*.

Summer

God's world's not made with human hands.
God's world's not what we "understand."
His world is greater, so-much-so
That we might miss it if we don't go . . .

Beyond the doors.

"It is finished," I'm sure He said,
When He created this big world for man.
While inside the doors, many things wait
To be finished at some future date.

Outside the doors are different sounds—
Maybe more, but yet they resound
With peace and love. He's nearer there.
I only know I have not a care . . .

Beyond the doors.

As God-thoughts rule, He lifts me high.
I exhale mundane, and inhale the sky.

So why not leave the "world" behind
At every chance you get?
And you may find, as I have now,
A world you won't forget . . .

Beyond the doors.

The Oak Trees

I had just gone out to the back porch and, as my mind and body were acclimating to awake-time, my gaze stopped on two trees. Oak trees! Why hadn't I noticed them before? The house had been here for more than two years. I had looked that direction many, many times before. Oak trees are rare in this area; however, with seventeen acres of trees, a creek and deep valleys, oak trees were "transplanted" here and nurtured by God until they reached maturity. Other large oaks are located in other spots on the property.

How did I recognize the oak? Its trunk is straight, upright and solid with a yellow hue that you will also see in its lumber, woodwork and furniture. Its crown is rounded—nearly a perfect sphere. The oak is a favored, substantial tree. Had I lived one hundred and fifty years ago, if an oak were available then, my husband might have cut it to make me a fine and usable piece of furniture.

I believe I see two oaks side-by-side! One is a bit bigger, but both are strong and straight. The larger Daddy tree shoots directly into the crown and the Mommy tree branches one direction, holding her crown of leaf-children. Both are immovable—firm in love, first for each other, and then for their children, and finally, for others—also firm in faith, in duty and in sacrifice.

Oak Leaves

God has seen your sacrificial giving to your spouse and He is well pleased. He has seen you stand upright next to him sharing the load, when you would rather be a light and leafy branch in his arms, being carried by him. Your strength is a shining example to all your children.

Gal. 6:9 And let us not be weary in well doing: for in due season we shall reap, if we faint not.

A Different World

I t is morning. I slept in a little and noticed my thoughts were in neutral when I awoke, not scattered and jumping from one topic to another as they often do. Neutral is a more peaceful state of mind.

First I called Eli, text messaging, "I luv u," and then I put his clothes in the dryer while the water was heating for my coffee.

When the coffee was ready, I walked out the sliding doors to sit in the sun on the north porch.

A different world.

Those panes of glass divided my moment in two. On one side—the hum of the dryer, the stagnant air, my work, thoughts of the day's tasks, the morning chores; and on the other, birds, katydids, insects, refreshing air, distant vehicles, and . . . *God.*

Although I had just awakened from restorative sleep, this was my time of mental and spiritual restoration and preparation. Oh how much better absolutely everything goes, when I take my time in this quiet place.

Come away with me, my love.

The art of being happy lies in the power of extracting happiness from common things. —Henry Ward Beecher

Song 2:13 Arise, my love, my fair one, and come away.

Eastern Kingbird

This morning I saw a bird that looked like a robin, except instead of the typical red breast, his was white. I also noted a white band at the end of dark tail feathers. I checked the guides that I have and decided that it might be an Eastern Kingbird. Then I visited Internet sites to verify that this species would be in Nebraska at this time of the year and found that Nebraska is a favored nesting state (along with North Dakota, South Dakota and Kansas). I also found the most popular breeding area here to be forested areas. The egg-laying period is from early- to mid-June, and the majority of nests are in cottonwood and willow trees. These factors confirmed this bird's identity. I also found that Eastern Kingbirds have been observed to line their nests with rose petals. Because of the cattle and wildlife here, rose bushes are about the only thing I planted that survived. Pink roses climb up the trellis and others are beginning at the bottom of the arbor. Two shrub roses cascade down the hill.

I saw this Kingbird on June 13, 2006, and in my Internet searching found this:

On the morning of June 13, 1943, the writer was watching an Eastern Kingbird as it sat on a telephone wire a few feet away. Suddenly it dove viciously at one of the outer blossoms of a huge rosebush bearing large, white flowers. It returned to the wire with a prominent white object in its beak which was assumed to be a captured moth. This it dropped, and quickly

plunged again at the white flowers, coming up with a larger beakful, and loosing a gleaming shower of petals. It flew some thirty yards to the top of an apple tree and there busied itself. Soon it returned to the wire above the bush, and the diving on the blossoms was repeated. This was again followed by a beak-filled rest on the wire and then a trip to the same tree. Suspicions that the kingbird might be using these white petals as nest material prompted an investigation. In the upper branches of the apple tree there was found a nest which was lined with literally dozens of the petals. Many were white and absolutely fresh; others were in various stages of dying and becoming brown as they progressed outward. This indicated that the petal-gathering probably had been in progress several days prior to June 13th. Sixteen attacks on the blossoms, followed by trips to the tree, were observed during the course of the day. It was noted that two other rose bushes on various parts of the premises were likewise visited. One of these possessed pure white flowers, as did the first, while the petals of the third bore just the faintest traces of pink.

A. C. Bent, "Life Histories of North American Fly-Catchers, Larks, Swallows, and Their Allies," Bulletin 179 (U.S. Nature Museum, 1942).

Line Your Nest with Rose Petals

- Keep a sweet spirit—pray.
- Love, love, love!
- Decorate your home with the fruit of the Spirit—gentleness, etc.
- Keep peaceful order in your days . . .
- . . . and in your home!
- Beautify the outside too—yourself, and your home.

God Plants My Garden

ast year I planted about twenty shrubs and several perennials. The cattle ate some of the shrubs, while the rabbits ate the rest (except for the roses). Other perennials are blooming this year along with God-planted wildflowers. Last year while weeding I left the colors and types I wanted, such as a purple ground cover by the steps to the lower level entrance, and a taller species lining the walkway by the arbor and near the "me-planted" flowers. I'm finding that landscaping is a partnership, and what a partnership! The Creator not only walks with me and talks with me in "the garden," He has been the Master Designer.

I love it!

I love the results of His handiwork. It is beautiful, and so much better—to me—than any man-made design.

In a like manner, we should walk and talk with our Creator in the garden of our homes and families. Let him be the Master Designer. Let go of the need to have the "last word." His design is so much better than ours.

Growth itself contains the gems of happiness. —Pearl S. Buck

The Petal Heart

A few days ago I brought some roses into the house and placed them on the kitchen table. This morning when I first got up, after looking out the patio door, I noticed a pink heart on the floor—a heart-shaped rose petal. It was a message from God, and *oh!* how I needed it today. He said to me:

Heb. 13:5 I will never leave thee, nor forsake thee.

Matt. 28:20 lo, I am with you alway, even unto the end of the world.

Rom. 8:35-39 Who shall separate us from the love of Christ? shall tribulation, or distress, or persecution, or famine, or nakedness, or peril, or sword? As it is written, For thy sake we are killed all the day long; we are accounted as sheep for the slaughter. Nay, in all these things we are more than conquerors through him that loved us. For I am persuaded, that neither death, nor life, nor angels, nor principalities, nor powers, nor things present, nor things to come, nor height, nor depth, nor any other creature, shall be able to separate us from the love of God, which is in Christ Jesus our Lord.

In this life, children will leave us, friends may leave us, spouses may leave us or die, beloved parents and others will depart as death separates us, but Jesus will *never, ever* leave us. What's more, he has perfect, unconditional, never-ending, forgiving, *forever* love for us. (So why, then, do we give Him so little time and our other relationships so much time?)

Thank You Lord for such a huge message about Your huge love in such a tiny petal!

The Hollyhock

I love "old-fashioned," I love cottage gardens, I love hollyhocks! I was so surprised yesterday morning as I saw, directly in front of the porch, a pink flower on what I thought was a weed! Funny, how I had left that plant there, although I had pulled many weeds after a recent rain. I had wanted hollyhocks but never planted any yet! Where did that hollyhock come from? *I know.* It came from my God—a special gift and a miracle just for me. He knows what I like and He blessed me.

He knows you.

Hollyhock

He knows you, inside and out. He knows both the good and the "bad" and he loves you anyway, and wants to bless you with special "hand-picked" gifts.

He knows what will bring you joy. In order to love completely, to love unconditionally, one must know the other completely, and He does. There are no secrets because He knows everything about us, but closeness can be broken.

Don't break that bond with God. Know God by spending time with Him. Reveal all your secrets to Him. Lay down your concerns and allow Him to lift your burdens. Get to know Him. He knows you and wants to spend time with you.

Read: Psalm 139

The Daylily

The bright orange Daylily blossom lives for only one day. As the sun rises, the bud opens and graces us with perfection and beauty for one day only.

In the same manner the Son rises on each of our days and graces it with His love, provision, beauty and other good things. Our job is in recognizing and being thankful. He created a beautiful flower that most people never even take time to notice. Consider how much more He cares for you this day.

Rest in that love, knowing today is good and even better days are directly ahead. This thought, of God's immense love, is bringing tears to my eyes even as I write it today. We all so need Him and His love in these daily doses and they can be huge daily doses! Expect them today!

Ps. 68:19 Blessed be the Lord, who daily loadeth us with benefits, even the God of our salvation. Selah.

Luke 11:3 Give us day by day our daily bread.

Matt. 6:34 Take therefore no thought

Daylily
Hemerocallis fulva

for the morrow: for the morrow shall take thought for the things of itself.

His Gifts

H as anyone by fussing before the mirror ever gotten taller by so much as an inch? If fussing can't even do that, why fuss at all? Walk into the fields and look at the wildflowers. They don't fuss with their appearance—but have you ever seen color and design quite like it? The ten best-dressed men and women in the country look shabby alongside them. If God gives such attention to the wildflowers, most of them never even seen, don't you think he'll attend to you, take pride in you, do his best for you? (Luke 12: 25-28, *The Message*)

Care for You

1 Pet. 5:7 Casting all your care upon him; for he careth for you.

Love for You

John 15:13 Greater love hath no man than this, that a man lay down his life for his friends.

Blessing for You

Luke 12:32 Fear not, little flock; for it is your Father's good pleasure to give you the kingdom.

What I'm trying to do here is get you to relax, not be so preoccupied with getting so you can respond to God's giving. People who don't know God and the way he works fuss over these things, but you know both God and how he works. Steep yourself in God-reality, God-initiative, God-provisions. You'll find all your everyday human concerns will be met. Don't be afraid of missing out. You're my dearest friends! The Father wants to give you the very kingdom itself. (Luke 12: 29-32, *The Message*)

Eugene H. Peterson, *The Message,* Copyright © 1993-2006

Letting God Do It

Sometimes day-to-day life and its busyness is an escape from heart issues. Then a day comes when it seems your nose is against a brick wall. Today was like that. I walked down the hill to the flagstone bench and sat facing backwards, nose to nose with the lavender flowers of a vetchling. I again noticed intricate detail that only the Great Designer could have created but the tears continued.

What was I going to do?

Then a butterfly landed. Its movement arrested my focus on self.

What is he going to do?

Look at the geometric pattern on his back and the shimmering metallic tones.

Immediately the tears stopped.
Like the butterfly, God is always moving, and we can expect Him to act and meet our deepest needs. We don't have to do anything, but just rest in His doing.

Hoary Vetchling
Lathyrus polymorphus

2 Chr. 20:17 Ye shall not need to fight in this battle: set yourselves, stand ye still, and see the salvation of the LORD with you, O Judah and Jerusalem: fear not, nor be dismayed; to morrow go out against them: for the LORD will be with you.

1 Sam. 17:47 And all this assembly shall know that the LORD saveth not with sword and spear: for the battle is the Lord's, and he will give you into our hands.

Cut The Dead Trees Down

Why do my eyes keep returning to the few dead trees amongst the verdant woods? Why are they drawn to these most unsightly parts of a beautiful view? Is it because of the contrast of the light brown against the rich green? Or is it the desire that all be perfect in my view *and in my life?*

When we begin to do this, when we notice the negative, the dead, the dying in our lives, we can "cut it down" and get it out of our lives. We can live "above the world," and be the overcomers we were meant to be. I count it a compliment if someone comments about my faith, optimism and trust in God, by saying, "You are not living in the real world," because that is exactly how we are supposed to live—above it all, as children of God.

Yes, there are days when it seems all we can see are the "dead trees." For me those days are usually days when I have not slept as much as I should the night before. However, we should never, day-after-day, focus on the negative, the things that need changing. Even though it sometimes takes effort, our focus needs to shift away from the "dead trees" to the green and growing. Even if it begins with a small thing, see it, and thank God for it.

The dead trees just remind us of what we don't want. Decide what you do want, and start directing your thoughts there. Look at the green and growing things. There are many in your life—yes, far more than the dead and dying things.

1 John 5:4,5 For whatsoever is born of God overcometh the world: and this is the victory that overcometh the world, even our faith. Who is he that overcometh the world, but he that believeth that Jesus is the Son of God?

John 17:15, 16 I pray not that thou shouldest take them out of the world, but that thou shouldest keep them from the evil. They are not of the world, even as I am not of the world.

He Loves Me!

How often do we really look at how much God loves us? I did today. *He loves me, He loves me not, He loves me, He loves me not.* When young, we would pluck petals off daisies to discover the verdict.

He loves me!

How do I know? I put my nose up to a Purple Vervain wildflower. It is everywhere this year! Our Joepyeweed will bloom soon and we have lots of it, too. I also investigated another plant that I call "Arms of God." It is mostly green with white edged leaves. One small flower is nearly hidden and protected in the center of four slightly larger flowers. He loves me!

He loves me not.

Don't we sometimes feel like we are far from God's love? Sometimes we just don't feel worthy.

"Arms of God"
Snow—On—The—Mountain
Euphorbia marginata

33

How could He possibly love me?!

Yet we are told that nothing shall separate us from His love, goodness and blessing . . . unless we let it! Greater God sees us through the perfection of His Son, and through the offering of His Son who make *us* "perfect."

He loves me!

Rom. 8:31-39 What shall we then say to these things? If God be for us, who can be against us? He that spared not his own Son, but delivered him up for us all, how shall he not with him also freely give us all things? Who shall lay any thing to the charge of God's elect? It is God that justifieth. Who is he that condemneth? It is Christ that died, yea rather, that is risen again, who is even at the right hand of God, who also maketh intercession for us. Who shall separate us from the love of Christ? shall tribulation, or distress, or persecution, or famine, or nakedness, or peril, or sword? As it is written, For thy sake we are killed all the day long; we are accounted as sheep for the slaughter. Nay, in all these things we are more than conquerors through him that loved us. For I am persuaded, that neither death, nor life, nor angels, nor principalities, nor powers, nor things present, nor things to come, nor height, nor depth, nor any other creature, shall be able to separate us from the love of God, which is in Christ Jesus our Lord.

Peter Rabbit

A crop duster woke me early as it circled and recircled over an adjoining quarter of land. I arose, made my coffee, dressed and went out to the back porch for my quiet time. As I sipped, and blue jays flew into the trees above, a young bunny peeped out from the high end of the hollow about twenty feet from the porch and began nibbling his breakfast.

I sneezed twice and even talked to him, but he didn't mind. Scotty, our Scottish terrier, looked at Peter but decided against his usual noisy chase. Still no movement. Then Scotty shook his collar. His tags resonated and Peter took off around the edge of the hollow down the narrow path.

Our enemy might come around and attempt his tactics on us, but nevertheless and always "we are more than conquerors." The enemy only comes as close as we let him come. He really has no right to try any of his dirty tricks on us! We have been given every weapon to defeat him and keep him away. We only need to believe this in our hearts and see him run down his "bunny trail" just as Peter Rabbit did when he heard the rattling of Scotty's tags. When our enemy hears

Purple Poppy Mallow
Callirhoe involucrata

the roar of the Lion of Judah—the words of the Son of God—how much more quickly will he flee!

2 Cor. 10:3-5 For though we walk in the flesh, we do not war after the flesh: (For the weapons of our warfare are not carnal, but mighty through God to the pulling down of strong holds;) Casting down imaginations, and every high thing that exalteth itself against the knowledge of God, and bringing into captivity every thought to the obedience of Christ . . . .

Our Shepherd

The pastures are knee-high and lush due to the frequent rains. The cattle graze contentedly coming closer to the house each day. Some even stand their ground against Scotty. He then turns and nonchalantly walks away as if he is saying, "I don't really want to chase cows today."

The Lord is my Shepherd.

These cattle are independent, "self-sufficient," God-dependant creatures. They even graze during the heaviest rainfall with nary a thought for cold or wetness. They take no thought for the storms. *Neither should we.* When we trust, we can "be asleep in the boat," even in the strongest storms.

The Lord is my Shepherd.

A shepherd takes care of his animals so that they need take no thought for themselves—what they will eat, what they will drink or when they will rest.

Sometimes he maketh them to lie down in green pastures. Then they rise again and graze. They graze directly in front of them, one inch at a time, one day at a time, enjoying the lush pastures their shepherd has led them to.

Because the Lord is your shepherd, you do not have to be in want. As the cattle do, just trust in God's love and provision.

It's Okay

Ezra has been roofing on ninety-degree days with a small business owner, the two of them taking a siesta during the hottest part of the day. Will Ezra go to college? No. Probably not, unless sometime in the future. *It's okay.* His thoughts are *Army.* In fact he wore his Army T-shirt during the figure-eight race that he entered for the first time at our county fair. While we excitedly watched from the bleachers, he came in third out of seven cars. Both Ezra and Eli have been working on their cars for months. Eli is entering the demolition derbies this year. My sons don't always appear to be the perfect Christians I would like them to be. *It's okay,* because I realize that things are not always as they appear to be. Often, we do not know the real meaning of what we see. God is always moving mightily, so *it's okay!*

Zephi is going back to Bible college next month after a year's sabbatical, working locally with her church. After a trip to Peru, she is even more determined to follow God's will for her life, which is cross-cultural ministries. She says she is totally open to God's leading anywhere in the world. Ohio, where she attends Bible school, is too far away in *my* opinion! But *it's okay.*

What's going on in your life? It's okay! God is in control. All is well, it really is. Simply believe Him and soon you will see the answer!

Prov. 3:5, 6 Trust in the LORD with all thine heart; and lean not unto thine own understanding. In all thy ways acknowledge him, and he shall direct thy paths.

Draw Near to God

I was on the back porch. In a few minutes' time, the sun rose in its July strength despite the cloud cover. My quest for the last two days has been drawing near to God. I have been reminded that this is the answer to everything, especially our need for love and intimacy.

Yesterday, I began that quest and, yes, the day had been better. This morning I awoke after really sweet dreams—at peace with God and totally rested.

How do we get close to God?

Open the Bible first of all. Began a notebook of the verses about God's nature such as, "Nevertheless I am continually with thee." (Ps. 73:23)

I moved to the other side of the house, to catch the breeze and avoid the direct sunlight. Like the brightest sun, God's pure brightness burns away any chaff in our lives. This is one result of getting close to God. Oh, how we need this! Oh, how we need to be purified and changed! Oh, what blessed peace results.

Daylily
Hemerocallis fulva

Ps. 73:25 Whom have I in heaven but thee? and there is none upon earth that I desire beside thee.

Ps. 73:28 But it is good for me to draw near to God: I have put my trust in the Lord GOD, that I may declare all thy works.

John 1:18 No man hath seen God at any time; the only begotten Son, which is in the bosom of the Father, he hath declared him.

The Black Bird

By Jean Hall

We were sitting on a bench in the middle of the city, enjoying a respite after shopping, when we noticed the bold, black bird. His objective was lying in the street: a discarded heap of French fries, sticking out of their paper container. When there was a lull in the traffic, he flew down, strutted a circle around the fries, cocking his head as he thought things over. We thought he'd just settle down to gobbling the treat, but there was more to this bird. . . . At last he began pecking at the potato strips, not swallowing any, but pecking them into pieces. We watched in fascination as he reduced the fries remaining in the bag to precisely sized bits. He was interrupted several times by passing cars, but always returned to the task, not eating, but chopping up into bite-sized pieces.

When at last his task was through, he took up one or two of the pieces in his beak, and flew away. A few moments later he was back for more, and back and forth he flew, scooping up tidbits and carrying them away, until the tattered paper blew empty.

We were reminded of the prophet, led into the wilderness, fed by ravens bringing bread and meat. Even in the midst of famine, in a dry place where there was no food to be had, God took care of him.

As we can trust He will care for us.

1 Kin. 17:1-6 And Elijah the Tishbite, who was of the inhabitants of Gilead, said unto Ahab, As the LORD God of Israel liveth, before whom I stand, there shall not be dew nor rain these years, but according to my word. And the word of the LORD came unto him, saying, get thee hence, and turn thee eastward, and hide thyself by the brook Cherith, that is before Jordan. And it shall be, that thou shalt drink of the brook; and I have commanded the ravens to feed thee there. So he went and did according unto the word of the LORD: for he went and dwelt by the brook Cherith, that is before Jordan. And the ravens brought him bread and flesh in the morning, and bread and flesh in the evening; and he drank of the brook.

Change

I t was the first cool day after the heat of the summer broke, and my first walk in a long time. I had been too busy, and it had been too hot, even to think of getting away from my cool lower-level office. Creating a book seems to take so many intensive hours, and after a tedious day working on an index, I began my walk down into the meadow.

The air was comfortable, bordering on cool. Startled birds scurried from the creek bed. They had been used to their privacy since no one had been around lately. They were used to having it all to themselves.

What a beautiful little snapshot of a view! I had not noticed that before! Look at that dead tree over there. No, it's just a large branch. There's another dead tree up the creek. There are goldenrods along the creek. It's been too hot and dry for them elsewhere. Oh! and look at that beautiful yellow flower! What exquisitely shaped petals! Everything looks so different! Where there were once thistles, now there are yellow, blooming sandburrs. The trees even sound different. The leaves are rustling.

Bigroot Prickly Pear
Opuntia macrorhiza

Change.

Everything changes! Nature is in a continual state of change. It is a natural thing. Why, then, do we fight it so? With faith and trust in God, our changes will be perfectly normal and improve our lives, and because there is one thing that doesn't change, we have the stability we so desire in our lives.

Mal. 3:6 For I am the LORD, I change not.

Wild Turkeys Teach

A wild turkey family grazed down the hill as I sat on the porch swing this morning. They were slowly relishing their breakfast of bountiful grasshoppers. The adults occasionally stretched their heads high looking for danger and direction, and then dipped low again for the insect feast. As they circled the house I continued to observe. All of the turkeys remained in a group. Although they sometimes grazed in opposite directions, they stayed together. I did not see the young in a separate classroom. No, the parents were teaching by example, alongside the young—one with them. *Together.*

They had been perfectly silent and then I heard a light "cluck." "Come this direction," she seemed to say, gently leading. Half went on one side of the obstacle (a cedar tree) and half on the other, all eventually crossing the drive and coming together again.

We gently lead our young and even if they go another direction for a time as they get older, we can trust that they will rejoin us, if we keep strong in faith and in sowing love in their lives.

Happiness is the realization of God in the heart, happiness is the result of praise and thanksgiving, of faith, of acceptance; a quiet, tranquil realization of the love of God. —White Eagle

Morning Guilds the Skies

I arose before dawn and grabbed my Bible, a notebook, pen, highlighter, hymn book, sweater, an afghan and coffee, and went out on the back porch. First pink, then yellow, soon the sun arose in pure unviewable golden light.

When morning guilds the skies, my heart, awaking cries, "Let Jesus Christ be praised."

I will not look back, obeying the command to forget the things that are behind. However, there are some areas in my life that I know need a touch of discipline. Yet I still resist, and have for years.

Just as I have learned to choose food that keeps me from gaining weight, I can do the right thing in these other areas. It starts with a firm, unwavering decision. Then God enables as we lean on Him and choose to do whatever it is that He wants us to do.

Phil. 4:13 I can do all things through Christ which strengtheneth me.

Decide to be Happy

You can decide to be happy. These things will also help.

♦ Get adequate sleep. It can make a huge difference in your outlook.

♦ Spend a lot of time in the Word, copying or marking scriptures to stand on. God wants only good for you!

♦ Eat right.

♦ Think positive thoughts, speak positive words. Decide you will not let anything negative stay in your thoughts or come out of your mouth.

♦ Journal—thank God in writing for current and future blessings, no matter how you "feel."

Decide that joy is the hue you want your heart to be. Then start making the little and large choices that over time will paint your heart happy. —Thomas Kinkade

Birds, Sun, Quiet and Money

I slept late today. I am on the porch that wraps around the very back of the house. Bird songs, sun on my feet and legs, and soft air laden with the "silent" sounds of bee buzz, breeze and distant vehicles lift my heart to God. *How can I be so blessed?* I have learned in the sharp and precise reality of this moment be content in whatsoever state I am in.

You are not your bank account balances. You are not your net worth. You are who you really are—a daughter of a mighty, powerful and very rich Father.

As our thoughts dwell on the richness of our lives, more richness will naturally and easily flow toward us.

Prov. 23:7 For as he thinketh in his heart, so is he.

Fall & Winter

♦ *Do you think this world is only an entertainment for you?*

♦ *Who can open the door who does not reach for the latch?*

♦ *Well, there is time left—fields everywhere invite you into them.*

♦ *Quickly then, get up, put on your coat, leave your desk.*

♦ *Listen, are you breathing . . . just a little, and calling it a life?*

♦ *Now the sun begins to swing down. Under the peach-light, I cross the fields and the dunes.*

I climb, I backtrack.
I float.
I ramble my way home.

Roger Housden, selected lines from "Have You Ever Tried to Enter the Long Black Branches," *Ten Poems to Set You Free* (New York: Harmony Books, 2003), p. 65.

Sometimes, It's Fall

I like Fall least. I see drabness, dying and cold. I don't see the golds and yellows that my Fall baby, Jessica, so loves. I don't see freshness and newness and color. I don't see snow-white wonderland nor the blazing fire of winter. I don't feel the soothing heat of summer nor the warm beautiful nights.

I have felt Fall more than usual this year. Jessica is marrying, which cuts her off Biblically from her birth family. (Mark 10:7) Compounding "Fall" for me this year is the fact that Zephi also moved out recently.

Sometimes it's Fall.

Fall is a season that I have to put up with. In our lives, there are Falls we have to "endure," whether we like them or not. Changes come and we have to live through them. With God's grace, we can walk victoriously through them, with hope for new surprises in our own lives, as we let go of our children and allow them to have their own new adventures.

Prairie Goldenrod
Solidago missouriensis

Jer. 31:17 And there is hope in thine end, saith the LORD, that thy children shall come again to their own border.

Be Still

I t is mid-October. I am on the high cliff across the big valley from the house. I am sitting very still. The oaks cascade down the steep cliff, their golden leaves backlighted by the sinking sun. The air cools but magnetic earth will not release its hold of me. I sit, I pray, I do not move. I bask in the ethereal beauty.

Suddenly a squirrel, with an acorn in his mouth, darts toward me. I remain motionless as he put his front paws on my lap and begins his feast. Amazing! He continues to eat until finished, and then leaves.

James 4:8 Draw nigh to God, and he will draw nigh to you.

I had been going through some tough times, but only when I took the time to draw nigh to God, could He make His love known to me. The miracle of the squirrel's direct contact exhibited the very real, and always present, love my Father has for me.

Jer. 29:11 For I know the thoughts that I think toward you, saith the LORD, thoughts of peace, and not of evil, to give you an expected end.

God is always with you and always loving you. His thoughts about you are always full of love, peace, and only good for you, and for your future. As soon as you align your thoughts with His thoughts, you will see dramatic changes in your life!

I arose and headed back to the house, refreshed and restored and em-powered, knowing *all is well,* it really is.

Ps. 46:10 Be still, and know that I am God.

A Day Off

I walked toward the creek with my lawn chair, coffee and notebook, then sat down and wrote the following.

Perfect peace—both physical and spiritual. My Daddy is so extremely good to me. What exceptional care He takes of me.

Some think that I do not work, but building a business is perhaps one of the most difficult jobs. Let's face it, we women are programmed to be homemakers and to be taken care of. Well—husband or not—we *are* taken care of. Our Maker is our husband and will provide for us even better than our earthly spouses. It helps to realize our oneness with Him. "Two shall become one ." We are truly connected to the Almighty—mighty, prosperous God. We are related by blood and very, very close. He "sticketh closer than . . ." anything or anyone in our lives.

Puncture Vine
Tribulus terrestris

God is your Father, and your Husband, and He loves you like no earthly father or husband possibly could. He thinks you are beautiful and always will be. He loves you unconditionally.

The birds exhibit their joy in the change of seasons and even Scotty seems happier in his explorations. Now he sits at my feet, quiet yet alert, absorbing subtle sights and sounds. Now he again meanders down the hill.

Amazing love.

How rich we are in the amazing, unconditional love of our God.

Luke 12:22-28 And he said unto his disciples, Therefore I say unto you, Take no thought for your life, what ye shall eat; neither for the body, what ye shall put on. The life is more than meat, and the body is more than raiment. Consider the ravens: for they neither sow nor reap; which neither have storehouse nor barn; and God feedeth them: how much more are ye better than the fowls? And which of you with taking thought can add to his stature one cubit? If ye then be not able to do that thing which is least, why take ye thought for the rest? Consider the lilies how they grow: they toil not, they spin not; and yet I say unto you, that Solomon in all his glory was not arrayed like one of these. If then God so clothe the grass, which is to day in the field, and to morrow is cast into the oven; how much more will he clothe you, O ye of little faith?

Weekend!

The weather has been cooling and rainy for the past few days so I've had to have my quiet time indoors, but after the strong wind all night and with the sunshine today, I test the porches. The breeze is from the south, so I choose the north porch (it actually wraps around the northwest corner). Here I am not only protected from the wind, but there is sunshine from the east.

It is wonderful to be here.

I missed being outdoors. I have been so busy with last-minute book production, that I have been under some stress. But now, I decide to *drop it* and not pick it up again. I also drop my pen . . . for even this notetaking could be defined as work when one is a writer.

It is restoration time.

I walk away from my pen and notebook, down the hill to the stone bench. Just me, the wide sky and . . . *God.*

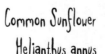

Common Sunflower
Helianthus annus

Peace descends, surrounds and settles. I go beyond the bench to the creek, and I sit down. Immediately, unfinished tasks began to flood my mind.

No, I say, as I turn my thoughts to the *now*—the air, the wind, the lowing cattle, the sun, the view of the creek and beyond.

God is everywhere.

I remembered my very strong revelation from yesterday, when this childhood fact seemed to be expanded a thousand times to me. He really is everywhere.

He is in the air, in the trees, in the wind, in my bank accounts, in my cells, in my DNA, in my future, in my past, in my present—*oh, yes!*—in my present. In this precious "now" moment. However, He is also in those moments when my conscious mind is not thinking of His nearness.

Remember that God is present everywhere, even in the busy moments of your days. You will feel an amazing supernatural connection that you can only experience when you recognize Him in everything, everywhere.

If God is everywhere, and as we truly become one with that fact, we also naturally walk in peace and love, as He is peace and love.

The Squirrel

Nights are cool now. At the creek, stately goldenrods humbly bow before ground-hugging sticktights.

Lord, I praise you with my whole heart as we sit in holy oneness: You in me and I in You. This is God-time. In Your presence, time stands still. I bask in this heaven-time where domineering earthly schedules are dethroned.

I sit near my birdwatching tree. A squirrel is twelve feet from me in the branches of a cedar tree. He is so confident, so nimble on his feet, so sure. *Why?* I watch. He jumps to a leafless tree. Right before his quick jump, he takes a split-second glance ahead.

We, too, need to look ahead enough to take sure steps in the way we are to go—never to hesitate or worry, but merely to see where we are going so we do not stumble in the dark, or fall from the branch that we are on. Yet, always, we must allow God and His peace to rule over earthly schedules.

Col. 3:15 And let the peace of God rule in your hearts, to the which also ye are called in one body; and be ye thankful.

Rosinweed
Silphium integrifolium

Seasons

On this day I sense definite change. The leaves are now falling. The sky is an agitated gray, yet somehow bright sun makes its way through to shine upon yellow and fall-green trees. It is dramatic. From one day to the next, the seasons changed.

There are other changes too. For nearly five months, all through Summer (by the calendar), I had been in deep Winter. My two youngest children had both been spending much less time at home. Day after day, I cried in an empty nest—hopeless about both my present and my future, forgetting that the "God of all hope" could once again fill me with "all joy and peace in believing." (Rom. 15:13)

But now, contrary to the calendar and the natural indications, it was Spring again. I wanted to go work in the garden—surely, I thought, a warm day is around the corner! My motivation was back! I thanked God for bringing me back to Spring, even though the natural world said otherwise.

Ps. 74:17 Thou hast made summer and winter.

Draw deep from the sustenance of Almighty God, as the trees draw from the earth what they need to keep them alive. Get to know God again.

Proverbs 12:206 Whoso trusteth in the Lord, happy is he.

The Wilderness

We never have to stay in the wilderness long, before God brings us into the garden. We are merely passing through. As we open our Bibles and read, realizing this is *God's* voice, we hear clear and beneficial words. His words create wholeness in our lives as we walk in their truth and instruction. His words bring us quickly into the garden.

Is. 51:3 For the LORD shall comfort Zion: he will comfort all her waste places; and he will make her wilderness like Eden, and her desert like the garden of the LORD; joy and gladness shall be found therein, thanksgiving, and the voice of melody.

Hearing from God

Is. 50:4 The Lord GOD hath given me the tongue of the learned, that I should know how to speak a word in season to him that is weary: he wakeneth morning by morning, he wakeneth mine ear to hear as the learned.

Hoary Vervain
Verbena stricta

Others' Expectations

*Is. 50:9 Behold, the Lord GOD will help me; who is he that shall con-
demn me? lo, they all shall wax old as a garment; the moth shall eat
them up.*

Snowy Day, Late Winter

I t snowed all Sunday and every church in the area was closed. It was the biggest snow of the entire winter, and it was wet! The branches on the cedar trees drooped gorgeously. There was a foot on the ground and more in drifts. We caught three mice in the house - it was a *Snow Disaster Day* for those little fellows. Scotty refused to go out, even though he stood by the door and longingly viewed the scene.

It was a good day. We had our Sunday dinner and finished up some cleaning and dishes. I struggled to bend over (pre-Atkins) and lace up the only boots that would keep out the deep snow as I walked. I grabbed my long wool coat, knowing that it would keep me warmer than my down jacket. As I stepped out, the fresh and frigid air invigorated me.

Ezra and Eli were wrestling and rolling down the hill. I walked past, down to the creek. The dam was gone!

"When did that happen?" I asked myself. Then I remembered the summer-like days of the previous week and, before that, the big snows west of us in the Colorado mountains.

"It must have been the big snow melt that filled the streams," I thought.

Later we watched "Santa Claus" on TV and played *Phase 10*. I had talked to both girls at different times during the day. It had been a very good day.

God is so good. Each day brings new wonders. Teach yourself to be aware of, and thankful for, all He has provided—little ones, home, food, trees, whatever! Like icing on a cake, or snow on a spring day,

He loads blessing upon blessing!

Ps. 52:1 . . . the goodness of God endureth continually.

Ps. 68:19 Blessed be the Lord, who daily loadeth us with benefits, even the God of our salvation. Selah.

Blessed

Thank You, Lord, that I am blessed this day—body, soul and spirit. Thank You, Lord, that we are touched by the power of God in all we do and say, and that my children—this day—and throughout their lives, experience and know the incredible power of Your Holy Spirit. Thank You for protecting them everywhere they go, and keeping us all healthy.

God has made this beautiful day for you! You are so blessed this day, because He loves you. Keep on giving thanks, speaking the blessing on everything and everyone in your life, and your outlook will change. The result will be that your "realities" will change! Things are changing, have changed, even right now, whether you see the change yet or not. When you pray, believe you have the things your are praying for and you will have them!

Mark 11:24 Therefore I say unto you, What things soever ye desire, when ye pray, believe that ye receive them, and ye shall have them.

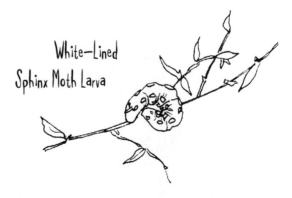

White—Lined
Sphinx Moth Larva

GOD

*5 That in every thing ye are enriched by him, in all utterance,
in all knowledge.*

Purpose

Everything we do is for the purpose of bringing glory to God, allowing His kingdom to come. Bringing our lives in line with His Word glorifies Him. We do not need to ask, "Lord, what is Thy will?" We know, if we know His Word. It is "righteousness, peace and joy in the Holy Ghost"!

This is the victory, even our faith.

When you fulfill your purpose you are worshipping God.

Mother's Heart

Christ identifies with a mother's heart and because He "came unto His own and His own (His children) received Him not," He *really* understands! What's more He is more than ready to comfort and make it all right.

Daughter of God!

The Lord is grace and truth, and we have received all of His goodness. It is our inheritance, passed "down" to us: "of His fulness have all we received . . . ." (John 1:16)

You are a child of God because you received Him; because you believe on His Name. You are a daughter of God! God really is your Father! What more do you need? He is provision! You are not an earthly child, coming from an earthly relationship. He chose you, creating you exactly the way He wanted you to be. Therefore you can be happy and blessed, without condemnation. If He does not condemn us, what right do we have to condemn ourselves?

1 John 3:1 Behold, what manner of love the Father hath bestowed upon us, that we should be called the sons of God.

John 1:13 Which were born, not of blood, nor of the will of the flesh, nor of the will of man, but of God.

Rom. 8:1 There is therefore now no condemnation to them which are in Christ Jesus, who walk not after the flesh, but after the Spirit.

Strength Attracts

I t was a long year. At the end of 2004 I decided I'd had enough. My broken and bleeding heart was going to heal. My life was no longer going to revolve around my children, who really didn't need me anymore anyhow. I decided to change.

Things arose that affirmed that I was an individual of worth, no matter how I had failed in the past, no matter how much criticism I had gleaned over the years and no matter that the "identity" of mother and teacher was no longer as real as it has been for so many years.

Jesus loves me.

That's all I needed to know. My life did the proverbial, and oh-so-real, "turn around." I untied the apron strings, took off the apron and even threw it out!

With God's help, 2005 did begin a new phase of my life. I set new goals and did a lot of journaling about what my new life would look like. Things in my heart, mind and life became more and more optimistic. I became remotivated to climb out of the rut I had been in, determined that I would began to walk on higher ground. I honestly no longer cared what my children thought of me, or how much love they exhibited or didn't exhibit. I was secure in God's love.

But guess what?

The relationship with each of my four children went to a new level. I freed them be what God wants them to be. They no longer needed to fight the invisible chains I had held them with. We began communicating more, and more peacefully.

If you have not yet come to this fork in the road, prepare now by—first of all—rejecting daily, any and all condemnation. Not always external, this can be internal and self-imposed or imagined. Bask in the love of God. Know that you are a very unique and special individual, and that your worth is not based on what you are doing (or not doing) now or will ever do (or not do). Take every "work" away and you are still valuable in the eyes of God. Reach out—get involved with people somehow, even for a few hours a week. Work or minister. No woman is an island. You need people and they need you. Maintain your friendships.

Zech. 4:6 Not by might, nor by power, but by my spirit, saith the LORD of hosts.

Rev. 3:8 I know thy works: behold, I have set before thee an open door, and no man can shut it: for thou hast a little strength, and hast kept my word, and hast not denied my name.

The End

What a gorgeous October day! The air was balmy and strong, yet oh-so-pleasant. I lay back and looked up. There was clearly a message from God in the sky. At least two jet streams crossed forming definite "kisses." The temperature was perfection itself. Eli's new puppy, "Chevy," was playing with "Grandpa Scotty," jumping over him and crashing on the other side. While Scotty lost patience, I laughed hilariously. Laughter is *so very* good. Somehow it seemed like *the end . . .* of summer.

The day continued in a special way, with the well-being of productivity as I completed pasting in all of my journal entries and began laying out this book.

When Zephi was packing to move out, I stayed in my room and cried all day.

Later, Eli came with his truck and some friends. I retreated downstairs to the office. Of course I do not want to see this! He has not been home very often lately, often sleeping in the big grain truck since he is working long hours during harvest season, but this is something else. He is moving out! This seems to be *the end.*

Scott E. Curry

I must avoid the feelings of loss as Eli moves out, and focus on the good things in my life and future.

Thank You Lord; my cousin called today and a friend called the day before yesterday. These calls lifted my spirits. We must keep in contact with people. God created us that way.

Heb. 13:16 But to do good and to communicate forget not: for with such sacrifices God is well pleased.

Blowing in from the Sea

By Jean Hall

How the wind did blow! I didn't remember hearing about high winds on the weather forecast, only a winter storm blowing in from the sea. And blow in, it did! There was supposed to be a trip to McDonald's that evening, eagerly awaited by our three-year-old, but one look out the window at the blowing trees and we were convinced that staying at home might be the better idea. And so we fried up some hamburgers of our own and sat to watch the "show" outside our windows.

There was a sapling directly across the street that was bent double in the wind gusts. We were certain that by morning it would have snapped in two, but when morning—and calm—arrived, the sapling was still there, pointing proudly to the sky.

On the other hand, many tall, proud trees had succumbed to the windstorm. There was no "going anywhere" that day, for all the roads in the area were blocked by fallen trees. Twenty-three trees had fallen along the route between our home and my husband's work! (Which was not far from the McDonald's restaurant, by the way. I'm so glad we decided to stay at home!)

The little sapling, young, soft and flexible, survived to grow, while great and towering trees were splintered and shattered by the wind. Somehow I am reminded of Jesus' words in Matthew 18, telling the disciples that they must humble themselves and be as little children to enter the kingdom of heaven. As we mature we become more set in our ideas, more "stiff-necked," less willing to bend our will to our

Maker's desire. May our hearts remain soft and in tune to His voice, that we might bend in the direction of His will and not be shattered!

Ps. 51:10-13 Create in me a clean heart, O God; and renew a right spirit within me. Cast me not away from thy presence; and take not thy holy spirit from me. Restore unto me the joy of thy salvation; and uphold me with thy free spirit. Then will I teach transgressors thy ways; and sinners shall be converted unto thee.

Jer. 18:1-6 The word which came to Jeremiah from the LORD, saying, arise, and go down to the potter's house, and there I will cause thee to hear my words. Then I went down to the potter's house, and, behold, he wrought a work on the wheels. And the vessel that he made of clay was marred in the hand of the potter: so he made it again another vessel, as seemed good to the potter to make it. Then the word of the LORD came to me, saying, O house of Israel, cannot I do with you as this potter? saith the LORD. Behold, as the clay is in the potter's hand, so are ye in mine hand, O house of Israel.

Spring

I heard God calling
And I came,
His Sun signalled me
With its flame.
His Wind called me
With its song.
His Birds said they had been waiting
Over long.
His little Brooks ran tumbling
Down the hills,
Luring me with laughter
Of rocky rills.
His Grasses, yellow-green,
Standing in the sun,
Held up their fingers
For me to come.
Heart of Oak and heart of Pine
Beat a faint tatoo—
Flowing sap in bole and bud
Climbing up anew.
Till at last the summons
Set my heart aflame—
I heard God calling,
And I came!

Edwin Osgood Grover

The Porch Swing

I can once again have my quiet time "out in the fields." It is the first warm day of the year. Cattle are lowing. Breeze is blowing. Birds are chirping and singing, while some are winging their way through ethereal air.

Native-prairie-grass ocean begins a few feet from me. My view from this select spot on the porch swing—depending on the time of year and of day—ranges from fireflies, the moon and stars in the night sky, to the daytime view of wildflowers and occasional wildlife. I've seen wild turkeys several times, and once I saw a solitary, usually nocturnal, coyote. I love the sunsets, but don't often rise early enough to see the sunrises. Dusk in the summer is gorgeous. Once I took a picture of immense white and fluffy "every-eye-shall-see-Him" clouds from this very spot.

Every eye will see Him and every knee will bow. What manner of "men" ought we be, then? Not only in keeping our lives right before Him, but also in leading others to Living Water so they can drink freely. This is our primary calling.

Phil. 2:10 That at the name of Jesus every knee should bow, of things in heaven, and things in earth, and things under the earth.

Rev. 1:7 Behold, he cometh with clouds; and every eye shall see him, and they also which pierced him: and all kindreds of the earth shall wail because of him. Even so, Amen.

John 4:11-14 The woman saith unto him, Sir, thou hast nothing to draw with, and the well is deep: from whence then hast thou that living water? . . . Jesus answered and said unto her, Whosoever drinketh of this water shall thirst again: But whosoever drinketh of the water that I shall give him shall never thirst; but the water that I shall give him shall be in him a well of water springing up into everlasting life.

Prayer

Prayer is not a religious ritual but should flow from relationship. Prayer is able to be accomplished always and without ceasing. Walk on through the storm, fire, pain, persecutions.

Know who you are. You are not a beggar. You are not a crumb eater. You don't need to weary God with praying, or wear Him down. Why would you, when it is "the Father's good pleasure to give you the kingdom"?

The prayer that pleases him is not begging, but walking in His Spirit, believing Him. He says, "I'll be there before you call My Name. Just believe I am Who I say I am."

You never need to continually *ask*. God is always ready to pardon. If you are fainting, you are not praying, and if you are praying you are not fainting.

Tall Hedge Mustard
Sisymbrium loeselii

Prayer means to wish forward, to desire toward an ultimate end, seeking those things which are above.

Now you are praying.

Neh. 9:17 But thou art a God ready to pardon, gracious and merciful, slow to anger, and of great kindness, and forsookest them not.

Ps. 8:3-6 When I consider thy heavens, the work of thy fingers, the moon and the stars, which thou hast ordained; What is man, that thou art mindful of him? and the son of man, that thou visitest him? For thou hast made him a little lower than the angels, and hast crowned him with glory and honour. Thou madest him to have dominion over the works of thy hands; thou hast put all things under his feet.

Dream Dreams

Five birds alight on the gigantic cottonwood, which is backlighted by the setting sun. Pink clouds melt into liquid gold behind its black silhouette. *Quiet.* All is more than quiet.

All is quiet within me. too. I begin to weep, overcome by God's goodness—His huge, overpowering, yet perfectly peaceful goodness.

Bask in His love. Dream dreams. Allow the blessings to come. He loves you so much!

Close your eyes and picture a place you're yearning to be. A place that is beautiful and comforting, where everything is hopeful and alive. —Thomas Kinkade

Shell Leaf Penstemon
Penstemon grandi florus

85

A Personal God

E ons ago the Great Flood settled in our valley, leaving deep sediment that even now produces lush beauty. *He did it for me.* I look out the second-floor window and view the greenest of green in the cup-like hollow below the cliff. Spring trees wave in the soft breeze— their dark branches still visible through soft yellow popcorn buds. The hills roll back towards the horizon, as to the strains of Bach. Five centuries ago, Bach was born—*for me.*

Father, You love me so much! I was in your thoughts long, long before I came to this earth, which you built for me.

Lest you think me arrogant, think again. What is a personal God, but One Who knows you from before time and loves you from before time and prepares wonderful gifts for you even before you arrive on this earth?

I walked down the knoll. A bunny hopped a few yards in front of me. He

Narrow-Leaved Puccoon
Lithospermum incisum

paused. I looked at his bright eye and talked to him. "You don't have to be afraid of me. I won't hurt you." God created that bunny *for me!*

After my stroll through the green, green meadow, I ascend back to the house—the house that God gave me so many years ago. Nearly one hundred years before that, Dr. Dickenson built this house *for me,* and even before that, God grew the trees for the lumber to build this house—*for me.*

Some years ago a landowner near here turned down nearly a million dollars for property adjacent to this place. The developers wanted to build a golf course. God was saving the natural views . . . *for me.*

Green Pastures

R est. God wants to see us refreshed and restored. To "lie down" in green pastures—just like our pastures this rainy spring. They provide lush sustenance for the cattle, and figuratively, lush restoration and sustenance for us.

I awakened refreshed and restored this morning, although I hadn't gone to sleep as early as I would have liked. I stretched and every part of my body felt rejuvenated, but my mind and my spirit, especially, experienced refreshing from the "wars" of the last couple days. I was at peace with God, knowing I had kept my mouth closed although others attempted to engage in battle. I had experienced the fruit of fleshy warfare previously and this R&R fruit was so much better.

The Lord is my shepherd.

It was as if I had lain in that green pasture all night, breathing in the restorative oxygen it produces. It was early. I looked to the window. Dawn was just beginning to break.

Dawn can be breaking in your life, even this very day. See beyond with faith-eyes. Go to bed with prayer and start your day early with prayer and time with God. Pray believing and enter into a good day where much is accomplished for His glory, and where you know—really know—that all is well.

Ps. 23:2 He maketh me to lie down in green pastures: he leadeth me beside the still waters.

1 Cor. 10:31 Whether therefore ye eat, or drink, or whatsoever ye do, do all to the glory of God.

Priorities

What is least satisfying to you? Is is housework, cooking, dishes? My least favorite activities are those that do not have a tangible or lasting result. But these chores must be done!

God's priorities—walking with Him throughout our days, recognizing our oneness with Him—will bring peace and order to our lives. His ways are so much higher and better and we will experience good as a result of yielding, submitting, resting and walking in His ways.

Is. 55:12 For ye shall go out with joy, and be led forth with peace: the mountains and the hills shall break forth before you into singing, and all the trees of the field shall clap their hands.

Is. 55:1-3 Ho, every one that thirsteth, come ye to the waters, and he that hath no money; come ye, buy, and eat; yea, come, buy wine and milk without money and without price. Wherefore do ye spend money for that which is not bread? and your labour for that which satisfieth not? hearken diligently unto me, and eat ye

Prairie Spiderwort
Tradescantia occidentalis

that which is good, and let your soul delight itself in fatness. Incline your ear, and come unto me: hear, and your soul shall live; and I will make an everlasting covenant with you, even the sure mercies of David.

Is. 55:8, 9 For my thoughts are not your thoughts, neither are your ways my ways, saith the LORD. For as the heavens are higher than the earth, so are my ways higher than your ways, and my thoughts than your thoughts.

Deep Roots

By Jean Hall

The weekend after a great windstorm, we went for a walk in the woods. Many of the great evergreens still stood, straight and proud, but whole groves had been devastated by the power of the wind, looking like a giant's game of pick-up-sticks. The wide, flattened-out root systems lay naked and impotent, thrust into the air as the trees fell. The area enjoyed generous amounts of rainfall, and as a result, the trees tended to be shallow-rooted. They didn't have to send roots down deep into the soil, seeking life-sustaining moisture. Theirs was an easy life, alternating sunshine and all the rain they could take in.

Faith tends to grow in the same way. When life is easy and we are showered with blessing, we might not pay much attention to heavenly things. It's too easy to get caught up in everyday demands and delights, and not even think of the Lord for hours, days on end. But it is when we are going through "desert times," though we might not even realize it at the time, that our faith is growing. We pray, we seek His face, if only to find relief in our suffering. Our roots go down deep, seeking the Living Water, enabling us to stand when the next windstorm comes.

Read 1 Pet. 4:12, 13

Free!

A yellow swallowtail butterfly circles outside the patio door. I am so, *so* thankful for the freedom I have in Christ alone! America is great because of God. America is free because of Christ. He is the one source of freedom!

Free to be me!

I do not have to fit into anyone's mold! He created me as a unique being and I am free to be unique, no matter how crazy my particular "unique" might be to others! *What a blessing*. It is like that butterfly—just released today to freedom. Freedom is a most precious, precious gift. I cherish it!

I am free, just like the female cardinal that I saw when I first awoke today, like the oriole couple that just flew by and like the robin out the window—we were *all* created to be free.

Spread your wings and fly.

Peace

Zephi, Ezra and Eli were here today—all together. It was so special!—love-filled, joy-filled and even flower-filled! We celebrated Zephi's and Eli's birthdays and Ezra's graduation. It was a blessed and peaceful day.

I am so glad that God looks deeper. I am so glad Jesus is not a hypocrite. I am so thankful that He loves the unlovable. I am so thankful that He provides peace always.

Thank You, Jesus, that You said, "There is no condemnation" Thank You, Jesus, that You love me unconditionally. Thank You so much, dear Jesus, for annihilating the work of the devil this day. Thank You, Jesus, for being more real to me this day—in hearing and answering my prayers. Father God, You are so good to me. I will praise and thank You always and You will turn things to good, always!

Rosinweed
Silphium integrifolium

Expect God to turn things to good in your life, even this very day. Expect the blessing. Expect Him to answer your prayers. Expect only good, for He is a very good God and loves you tremendously!

Still Waters

He leadeth me beside the still waters—and He doesn't make me drink, but simply presents clear refreshing water. We can choose it . . . *or refuse*. We choose to be refreshed or remain dry.

Have you ever become irritable when thirsty? I have! Another effect of thirst is lethargy. They say that daytime fatigue arises from this exact cause. When we have enough pure water, our cells are refreshed and become energized. Likewise abundant draughts of the water God offers us through His word and presence, keep us energized for our tasks, yet peaceful and calm in spirit.

He restoreth my soul.

As he restoreth my body in sleep, while breathing fresh air, He restoreth my soul through His still, peaceful, yet powerful water that I sip when reading His Word.

Ps. 23:2, 3 He . . . leadeth me beside the still waters. He restoreth my soul: he leadeth me in the paths of righteousness for his name's sake.

The heavens declare the glory of God; and the firmament showeth his handiwork. Day unto day uttereth speech, and night unto night showeth knowledge. There is no speech nor language, where their voice is not heard. Their line is gone out through all the earth, and their words to the end of the world. In them hath he set a tabernacle for the sun, which is as a bridegroom coming out of his chamber, and rejoiceth as a strong man to run a race. His going forth is from the end of the heaven, and his circuit unto the ends of it: and there is nothing hid from the heat thereof. (Ps. 19:1-6)

The Baby Cardinal

I found the perfect bird-watching spot. It is down the slope from the house, near a grouping of nine to ten medium-sized dead trees. The birds, in their early morning rituals, rest in the leafless branches. I brought binoculars and *The Spotter's Handbook* along with my quiet-time materials.

A young cardinal alights on the branch. How distinctive its little tuft of baby's crown!—not yet filled out, it stands up like the two to three feathers of an Indian headdress. Its breast is splotchy, part brown, part rust-red.

Not yet what it will be.

Not yet what *we* will be. "But when He appears we shall be like Him."

And there, for an instant, was the mature scarlet cardinal in all his glory, singing his glorious song. We will be changed as the corruptible puts on incorruptible. We too shall be like him—like our Father.

1 John 3:2 Beloved, now are we the sons of God, and it doth not yet appear what we shall be: but we know that, when he shall appear, we shall be like him; for we shall see him as he is.

Use Your Senses

Choose to use your senses more often, and more of them. Notice fragrances, and use fragrances such as flowers and candles. Fill your life with uplifting, relaxing music. Decorate with colors and items that bring you joy. Perfume your body and your bath. Sing and speak musical, loving words. Notice fragrant flowers in your landscape, and singing birds. Really taste your food, notice aromas and attractive arrangements.

Decide that joy is the hue you want your heart to be. Then start making the little and large choices that over time will paint your heart happy. —Thomas Kinkade

Wild Bergamot
Monarda fistulosa

Rushing Grasses

I t is blowing hard today. I walk down the hill and notice the prairie grasses, rushing, rushing, rushing in the wind.

Our lives are like that.

Each day is so busy that it seems like the speed of life is a million miles an hour. As we age, the days and years pass faster and ever faster, and yet it seems—as the song says—"every day with Jesus is sweeter than the day before." Even though it seems our lives are "swifter than the weaver's shuttle" or than prairie grasses blowing in high winds, like the grasses our roots are deep, we are unmoved.

Yet for some, although time may pass this way, they feel they are going nowhere, and making no progress. If that's you, you can trust God as well as ask Him for direction.

Begin to take inventories of your life, your dreams and desires. Both reading and writing can change your thinking, which in turn will change your life. Be open to wisdom. It all comes from God, and being Omnipotent God, He can use anything and anyone to bring you to the next level of faith in Him.

I praise You Jesus, in this quiet place. I expect to be filled with all I need to get me through a whole day of earth time, kept in perfect peace as my mind is stayed on you; as I carry this time, this union with You throughout this day.

Come Away

The noise of many voices call. Seventeen acres of buds *insist* I awake and begin my day. Does it seem like seventeen acres of human voices call out to you, look to you, not only to "arise and work" but for every need under the sun?

Wait.

Do you hear that one voice saying "arise, come away with me, my love"? Grab your coffee or tea, your Bible and your journal, find a quiet spot and prepare your inner woman with the supernatural peace that is louder than one thousand voices, and will carry you effortlessly through the day.

Thankfulness from Murmuring

Focusing on the good in your life, and thanking God in faith for the solution to the thing you are complaining about, will bring the change you need!

The Mother Tree

Hone my gaze
to the riches
of detail—
slight as the fur
on a bee's belly
or the veins, thin as breath,
lining a forgotten iris
translucent
as a wing—
rewards
the hasty eye
and anxious heart
do not recognize.

Katherine Mosby, *The Book of Uncommon Prayer* (New York: HarperCollins Publishers, 1996), p. 19.

The Mother Tree

Each morning during the cooler months, I sit in bed and have my quiet time. There is a tree directly in view outside my bedroom window, at the edge of the woods, that is perfectly shaped, except for a very slight leaning toward a tiny evergreen that hugs the base of its trunk. It is a fruit-bearing mulberry. I call it the Mother Tree.

Today I noticed that this tree is not one of the biggest trees in view. This Mother Tree, although shorter and smaller than others, looks stronger and steadier. It is not waving in the wind as the other trees of the wood are. Like the Mother Tree, although the "weaker" sex, we can be stalwart and strong; unshakable, and like the Mother Tree we can bear spiritual fruit. *Nothing to it.*

Look at the baby evergreen leaning into the Mother Tree. Like this evergreen, we can lean into God, allowing Him be our Mother, our Father, our Everything.

Let Him hug you tightly—protecting, shading and keeping you safe. Learn to lean toward living "in Him." Let Him be your habitation, your dwelling place.

Ps. 71:3 Be thou my strong habitation, whereunto I may continually resort: thou hast given commandment to save me; for thou art my rock and my fortress.

Ps. 91:9-15 Because thou hast made the LORD, which is my refuge, even the most High, thy habitation; there shall no evil befall thee, neither shall any plague come nigh thy dwelling. For he shall give his angels charge over thee, to keep thee in all thy ways. They shall bear thee up in their hands, lest thou dash thy foot against a stone. Thou shalt tread upon the lion and adder: the young lion and the dragon shalt thou trample under feet. Because he hath set his love upon me, therefore will I deliver him: I will set him on high, because he hath known my name. He shall call upon me, and I will answer him: I will be with him in trouble; I will deliver him, and honour him.

Bone of my Bones

The Mother Tree is a fitting example of motherhood and yet it isn't quite complete. Since the "children" are evergreen, while the "mother" is deciduous, it might be a better example of adoptive motherhood with the "offspring" different in some way from the mother. Natural motherhood is "bone of my bones, flesh of my flesh." For both adoptive and natural parents, it is painful when our children depart from us at adulthood. It is like part of us—*the part connected to our heart*—is being torn from us. From my perspective, "This, too, shall pass." You will become less connected and it will be less painful as the years go by. Yes, it might take several months or more, at least it did for me. Nevertheless, we should not live in the past, but rejoice in the present.

Focus on the good in your life and in your children's lives, and perhaps even start thinking about some dreams and goals of your own that have been on the back burner while you were raising your children. Make lists of what you want to do with the rest of your life. It is *un nuovo giorno,* "a new day" for you.

I painted this Italian phrase over the entrance to my home. It reminds me that God wants only good for me, now and in my future. I have seen good in my life since my children left. Doors have opened to new experiences that I did not even dream about when they were all home.

The heart connection to our children also enables us to pray in faith for them and see those prayers answered, even after they become adults. God never overrides free will but He can turn our children's wills back to Him, back to choosing things that please Him, if it seems they are going the wrong way. He can do anything!

Jer. 32:17 Ah Lord GOD! behold, thou hast made the heaven and the earth by thy great power and stretched out arm, and there is nothing too hard for thee.

Jer. 32:27 Behold, I am the LORD, the God of all flesh: is there any thing too hard for me?

Prov. 3:5,6 Trust in the LORD with all thine heart; and lean not unto thine own understanding. In all thy ways acknowledge him, and he shall direct thy paths.

Our Thoughts

One day I saw birds flying in and out of the green leafy crown of the Mother Tree. Do we let worried and negative thoughts "fly" in? We ought not.

Another day the very top of the tree was in sunshine, while the rest was not. Will we let the "Sonshine" flood our thoughts with his comforting, assuring words, and allow those words to change things in our lives?

Thoughts are extremely important. They are so important that your life is actually a result of your thoughts.

If all looks dark around you, take a thought inventory. Change your thoughts. Let your mind be renewed. Keep your "crown" full of the Word, full of gratitude and full of positive, joyous thoughts.

Think only on things that are:

- ♦ true
- ♦ honest
- ♦ just
- ♦ pure
- ♦ lovely
- ♦ of good report
- ♦ virtuous
- ♦ praiseworthy

Phil. 4:8

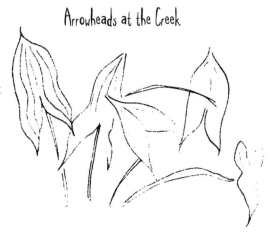

Arrowheads at the Creek

Prov. 23:7 For as he thinketh in his heart, so is he.

Immovable

The Mother Tree is not a prominent tree in the woods, but it is unique and distinctive. While other trees are larger and grander, the Mother Tree is shorter and less conspicuous. While the other trees are swaying in the wind; she is immovable, her leaves rustle not. She seems to be protected and sheltered, and yet she is at the very edge of the wood. I even see a tree directly behind her that sways, but the Mother Tree has innate stability. God knows *she needs it!*

The Mother Tree's littlest one is nestled under her "arms" while the older "children" are varying distances from her, yet always in sight. One little guy is farthest from her, although some "older" offspring stay closer.

Like the Mother Tree's children, our children each have unique personalities. Some of the younger ones seem to be bolder and more independent. These are the ones who, when grown, go off to war or become missionaries to China or other distant countries. Others may live nearby, but seem to be distant in other ways. Near or far, there is no distance in prayer, nor in the power of God.

2 Cor. 10:4 For the weapons of our warfare are not carnal, but mighty through God to the pulling down of strong holds.

Is. 49:25 But thus saith the LORD, Even the captives of the mighty shall be taken away, and the prey of the terrible shall be delivered: for I will contend with him that contendeth with thee, and I will save thy children.

Jer. 31:16, 17 Thus saith the LORD; Refrain thy voice from weeping, and thine eyes from tears: for thy work shall be rewarded, saith the LORD; and they shall come again from the land of the enemy. And there is hope in thine end, saith the LORD, that thy children shall come again to their own border.

Older Children

The light shines a little differently on the Mother Tree this morning. It is much brighter. Pale scraggly branches are here and there in her crown. Gray hairs? She is still green and flourishing. Her trunk-foundation is straight, only leans a little toward her "child-tree" who leans even more heavily upon her.

Although it seems older children do not need us anymore, they do. However, their needs are less for physical sustenance, than spiritual. They are about to go out into the world and face all of the challenges of life. *My, do they need us more!* They need us to be the unmoving, faith-filled and praying Mother Trees that they can lean into, even if in intangible ways. This is not the time to weaken or collapse in any area. We must continue to be strong for them, and we can be, as we lean into God and as He hovers over us, like the larger trees do over the Mother Tree.

Prairie Coneflower
Ratibida columnifera

Eph. 3:20 Now unto him that is able to do exceeding abundantly above all that we ask or think, according to the power that worketh in us.

Different but Similar

The Mother Tree is a hardwood tree. The "children" are cedars. Don't you sometimes feel like you and your children—especially your older children—are not related?

It is Fall. The Mother Tree has lost her crown, while the "children" are green and fresh—eager for new challenges. They thrive on springing faith, in aliveness, in movement.

The Mother Tree has lost her crown.

While the child-trees look like they are moving out into the world, the mother tree is anchored right where she is. Moving is not possible.

Our heart wants to run after our children when they begin to "detach" from us. We have a painful longing that they stay with us "just a bit longer." We begin to feel the emptiness of the once-full nest.

The Lord meets us in this place where we can do nothing but stand. We cannot run after them, to re-gather them as they begin to depart. No, our job is to stand strong, where we are. They will return in God's timing.

Eph. 6:10, 13 Finally, my brethren, be strong in the Lord, and in the power of his might. . . . Wherefore take unto you the whole armour of God, that ye may be able to withstand in the evil day, and having done all, to stand.

Think Green

Leaves are falling. After last night's frost, Fall's gold is fading to browns and olives, but the Mother Tree is still vibrant green. In fact, she is greener than any of the adult trees that surround her, the same depth of hue as her evergreen "children."

You can be a green tree in the "autumns" of your life. You can maintain stability, joy, hope and faith through it all. *How?* Feed on the deep spiritual nutrients of God's Word. "Think on these things." Bring your thoughts into captivity, because your thoughts create your reality. Stop being scatterbrained with fears and doubts. When God tells us to take our thoughts captive, He means we have to do something. We have to *choose* not to let negative thoughts rule our life.

God's creative power is within you. Right now, your thoughts are creating your future, and each child's, future, so make sure your thoughts are faith-filled and optimistic. *This is the essence of faith.* Replace bad thinking with

Buffalo Bur
Solanum rostratum

good thinking . Make sure that the thoughts you have are "creating" good for you and others. Make your thoughts line up with the Word, with your standards. Thoughts and resulting habits separate great men and women of God from the not-so-great.

When you change your way of thinking, you change your life. Everything about your life is a reflection of the way you think most of the time, or the way you have thought in the past. Change your habits of thought and change your future. Remember, you have a powerhouse within you!

Heb. 11:3 says: Through faith we understand that the worlds were framed by the word of God, so that things which are seen were not made of things which do appear.

2 Cor. 10:5 Casting down imaginations, and every high thing that exalteth itself against the knowledge of God, and bringing into captivity every thought to the obedience of Christ.

Phil. 4:8 Finally, brethren, whatsoever things are true, whatsoever things are honest, whatsoever things are just, whatsoever things are pure, whatsoever things are lovely, whatsoever things are of good report; if there be any virtue, and if there be any praise, think on these things.

Dried and Dead?

The Mother Tree looks like it is dried up, although green surrounds it. Is it naturally late in the leafing process? Some are. *Or is it dead?*

Yes, the mothering identity of my life is dead—it no longer defines who I am and I am very okay with it! How could I have imagined this place a few years ago? I truly thought it was the end of the world when my children left! Since then, I have been reminded that when we simply have faith in God, He takes care of everything about our lives.

Now I excitedly live my present, and look forward to my wonderful future. Truly every day with Jesus is sweeter than the day before. He takes off the limits! He breaks the walls! I am not only living my dream, but many more dreams are coming true for me.

Have faith! It is the key to super-victory in every area of your life. The best days of your life are just ahead. There is light at the end of the tunnel. This, too, shall pass.

Distressing things are really such a small part of our lives. We do best to ignore them, to focus on the good and the promising. We will be happier, more hopeful and see results much quicker!

Give love, and love to your life will flow, a strength in your utmost need; have faith, and a score of hearts will show their faith in your work and deed. —Madeline S. Bridges

1 John 5:4 For whatsoever is born of God overcometh the world: and this is the victory that overcometh the world, even our faith.

Eph. 3:20 Now unto him that is able to do exceeding abundantly above all that we ask or think, according to the power that worketh in us.

Be Thankful

My children are gone. True, Eli still sleeps here, but my mothering days are over and done. However, the Mother Tree is still here and this morning its crown is bathed in sunlight.

I am grateful that my children are responsible adults, and support themselves. The have all served others in various ways: Jessica in her position as a customer service manager, Zephi in her church and in missions work, Ezra serving God and country in Iraq and Eli, always willing to help others locally, including stopping to help stranded motorists or pulling people out of snow drifts.

What do you have to thank God for, about your children? Make a list. When you recognize those good things, and you will see more and more things in them to thank God for!

Phil. 1:3 I thank my God upon every remembrance of you.

Daisy Fleabane
Erigeron strigosus

New Growth!

The weather is cooling. So-much-so, that I am back to my quiet time spot on the bed with a view of the Mother Tree.

Although movement in the grass below the tree first caught my eye, I then looked at the tree's crown. It has the definite lighter green of new growth. This last spring I thought it dead, but now the Mother Tree clearly exhibits youth and health, while showing a capacity for many more productive years.

When my children left, they left. There was no turning back. The window of opportunity and the door of teachability closed. That chapter of my life was finished, and I had to turn the page to the next chapter, whether I wanted to, or not.

Listen, Mom, it's all good.

Just because you do not see the next chapter's title before you turn the page, just because you don't know what will unfold in that story, does not mean that there is something to dread or to be concerned about. Remember how much God loves you, and how His plans for you are all good!

This is once again where the trust factor enters our lives. I can

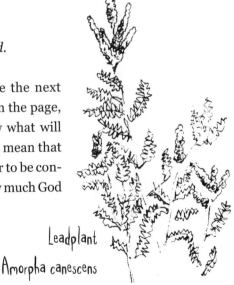

Leadplant
Amorpha canescens

testify from my own life: When the page is turned in faith, you will not be disappointed!

Jer. 29:11, 12 For I know the thoughts that I think toward you, saith the LORD, thoughts of peace, and not of evil, to give you an expected end. Then shall ye call upon me, and ye shall go and pray unto me, and I will hearken unto you.

Regrets

We all think things might be different if we could turn back time, but would they, really? When we know our entire lives, and our children's lives, are in God's mighty and capable hands, we do well to forget the past as we are told and to press forward with joy and expectation.

It is entirely possible to be happy in the "now" even if the "now" is not exactly what we would like. In fact, if you find things to be happy about right now, your future will be more to your liking.

Look around at all your blessings, and be happy now. Begin, also, to see your potential for new growth. God can turn your "messes" into miracles!

Heb. 13:5 Let your conversation be without covetousness; and be content with such things as ye have: for he hath said, I will never leave thee, nor forsake thee.

Phil. 3:13, 14 Brethren, I count not myself to have apprehended: but this one thing I do, forgetting those things which are behind, and reaching forth unto those things which are before, I press toward the mark for the prize of the high calling of God in Christ Jesus.

Happiness is a butterfly which when pursued is just out of grasp . . . . But if you will sit down quietly, may alight upon you. —Nathaniel Hawthorne

Call Unto Me

C ry unto Him, establish a serious prayer time, cry and call to Him for the biggest messes in the world and in your life and in your children's lives and He will answer you. *He will answer with good* and He will show you *great and mighty things, which thou knowest not* (Jer. 33:3). Why do we continually limit him?

When Ezra was in Iraq for a year, he carried out dangerous missions nearly every day. I prayed for his protection, but I also prayed for the protection of all the American forces, and especially for his entire company there. *They did not lose one man.* In fact, when they came back, they did not have enough room in the barracks because the Army had expected that some would not come back. This power of prayer was also reinforced strongly after he returned, when American deaths in Iraq increased greatly, reminding me to continue my praying.

I never feared for Ezra's life in Iraq. The Army was the best thing that happened to him, and definitely God's will, so how could I question it? The way I looked at it was, "If God could protect him on American soil for all the previous years of his life, and I knew *God* had, why could He not protect him in Iraq?"

Never limit God. Absolutely nothing is too hard for him.

Jer. 33:3, 6, 8 Call unto me, and I will answer thee, and show thee great and mighty things, which thou knowest not. Behold, I will bring it health and cure, and I will cure them, and will reveal unto them the abundance of peace and truth. And I will cleanse them from all their iniquity, whereby they have sinned against me; and I will pardon all their iniquities, whereby they have sinned, and whereby they have transgressed against me.

Thy Maker is Thy Husband

Married or not, we would do well to consider the Lord our true husband. As we form this intimate relationship with Him, other relationships improve. No husband can meet our heart's cry for complete unconditional love and intimacy anyway, although some may seem to come close (and all *should,* according to Christ's instructions to them).

When Christ is our husband, we will serve Him in an acceptable, pleasing manner, knowing He is worthy of our perfect service. Our daily duties are service to Him, even in our service to others.

When you really love someone, you have no problem submitting to him or serving him. That is a natural and deep desire, particularly if he loves you in return. *Oh! How He loves you and me!*

The supreme happiness of life is the conviction that we are loved. —Victor Hugo

Rom. 8:31 What shall we then say to these things? If God be for us, who can be against us? He that spared not his own Son, but delivered him up for us all, how shall he not with him also freely give us all things? Who shall lay any thing to the charge of God's elect? It is God that justifieth. Who is he that condemneth? It is Christ that died, yea rather, that is risen again, who is even at the right hand of God, who also maketh intercession for us. Who shall separate us from the love of Christ? shall tribulation, or distress, or persecution, or famine, or nakedness, or peril, or sword? As it is written, For thy sake we are killed all the day long; we are accounted as sheep for the slaughter. Nay, in all these things we are more than conquerors through him that loved us. For I am persuaded, that neither death, nor life, nor angels, nor principalities, nor powers, nor things present, nor things to come, nor height, nor depth, nor any other creature, shall be able to separate us from the love of God, which is in Christ Jesus our Lord.

136

OUR YOUNG FOLKS' JOSEPHUS
ANTIQUITIES OF THE JEWS AND THE JEWISH WARS

"Jump back in time to a place where historical accounts of the Hebrews are brought to life in an exciting narrative style. The history of Ancient Israel is revealed in a first-hand account from the great historian Flavius Josephus. OUR YOUNG FOLKS' JOSEPHUS is a compilation of his two greatest works, ANTIQUITIES OF THE JEWS and THE JEWISH WARS. You'll marvel at the history that is played-out before your eyes. A journey that begins with the call of Abraham and ends with the destruction of Jerusalem and the fall of Massada...this is a must-have for any bookshelf." ~ *Eclectic Homeschool Online*

This work is an invaluable supplement to the study of ancient Israel, covering a broad period of time in detail, yet at a pace suitable for the upper elementary and middleschool student. Beautifully illustrated with antique lithographic art.

PaideaClassics.Org

Also available at Amazon.com (Marketplace), Rainbow Resource, The Book Peddler, TanglewoodEducation.com, Arx Publishing and other fine homeschool retailers.

Homeschooling at the Speed of Life

Marilyn Rockett's latest book, Homeschooling at the Speed of Life (B&H Publishing Group, 2007), will be out April 1, 2007 and is available now for pre-publication purchase on www.Amazon.com.

Visit Marilyn's website at www.MarilynRockett.com or contact her at Marilyn@MarilynRockett.com.

SHADE TREE COTTAGE

www.shadetreecottage.com

Mineral salt baths
Botanical milk baths
Organic bath teas
Herbal goods

1-866-790-5091
shadetreecottage@comcast.net

Handcrafted Organic and All Natural Soaps